Computer Science for
IB Syllabus

HL & SL
Study Notes

Topic 1 System Fundamentals

Sarah Shakibi PhD

Head of Computer Science

Ellesmere College

Shropshire

UK

sshakibi4560@gmail.com

Contents

This volume is for Topic 1: System Fundamentals of the IB Computer Science Syllabus.

It is aimed at both teacher & learner.

The 'verb' for each specification point is very important and crucial to what is required in the learning and examination process.

The usual verbs which are used in examination questions are:

> ➢ Identify: to pick the correct answer
> ➢ Compare: to ensure more than one element is included in the answer usually with the use of advantages and disadvantages
> ➢ State: short and concise answer
> ➢ Explain: how it works
> ➢ Describe: what it looks like
> ➢ Discuss: the hardest which needs a logical comparison between advantages and disadvantages PLUS an intelligent conclusion

One of the main reasons why students systematically get low marks in questions is the lack of attention to the verb of the question.

It is recommended that teachers use this as their main focus in teaching the topics in order to maximise the learning and exam outcomes.

S/E refers to Social & Ethical considerations for a topic – these will invariably be different depending on where the syllabus is studied.

INT refers to the International aspect of a topic.

1.1 Systems in organisations

1.1.1 Identify the context for which a new system is planned.

New IT systems are being developed all the time in almost every type of organisation from a small shopkeeper who wants a custom built stock control system to the NHS who want a national database on which they can keep the medical records of every person in the UK.

Here are a few other examples of IT systems:

- Banks - customer record systems, systems for ATM machines, systems for approving or rejecting mortgage applications
- Hospitals - pharmacy systems for keeping track of drugs and creating printed prescriptions, appointment systems for outpatients
- Government - online tax payment system, online census information
- Supermarkets - stock control systems, payroll systems

A new IT system may be commissioned for a number of reasons:

- ➤ The current one is out of date and no longer doing its job effectively

- ➤ Technology might have moved on and new things are possible that couldn't be done with the previous system

- ➤ A competitor has developed a new system or process and the organisation needs something similar in order to offer the same service to customers

- ➤ The organisation has grown and the current system can't cope with the increased demands placed on it. Perhaps the company had only a few customers to start with but now it needs to be able to deal with hundreds of accounts.

- ➤ A new part of the company needs IT support e.g. a new customer service help desk.

- ➤ The company might want to improve the quality of a repetitive task. Doing the same thing over and over is very tiring and tedious for a person. A robotic system may be able to help with this. For instance the car industry makes heavy use of robots in their factories.

- ➤ The extent and limitations of a new system must always be judged and measured against the most fundamental concept of:

- ➤ Systems Analyst must identify:
    - o The various data inputs into the new system, data formats & validations required
    - o The various processes which will be performed on the inputted data
    - o The various outputs required from the new system

- ➤ Who uses the system and their user roles: end users and their various roles. If you are also doing Option A Databases then you can relate this topic by saying that various roles require various 'views' of the system and these all need to be identified clearly and become part of the initial systems analysis and overall objectives of the new system

LINK:
- ➤ How will the new system be installed: relate to topic 1.1.5 and various installation methods

- ➤ What will be the underlying infrastructure in terms of hardware & protocol: need to identify if the new system will be installed in a LAN or WAN and whether remote access from other geographical areas should be considered. The hardware and software protocol must be taken into consideration

- ➤ What bespoke outputs will the system produce which were not present before: often the new system is required mostly at managerial level and the bespoke reports (on screen or printed) are some of the most crucial outputs required by the system.

These usually rely on robust database query languages such as SQL and must be taken into consideration in the initial phase of systems analysis.

1.1.2   Describe the need for change management

"What if we don't change at all ...
and something magical just happens?"

www.torbenrick.eu

http://www.teach-ict.com/as_a2_ict_new/ocr/A2_G063/331_systems_cycle/slc_stages/miniweb/pg3.htm

- How change is managed is very important since it directly impacts employers & employees
- Important factors: Time, training, cost, method of change
    - How much time is available for the change over
    - How much training is required in order for the employees to be fully productive on the new system
    - Which method of change is being considered and why?
    - How much will the change cost from start to finish?

- Employees need to be trained and to be overseen as they take over the new system

- Management needs to ensure there is a seamless transition from old to new and user queries are dealt with efficiently and quickly.

- Without change management users would be left to their own devices and would naturally evolve at various paces through the new system. This would seriously affect the productivity of the new system which in turn impacts the employers business

1.1.3 Outline compatibility issues in situations including legacy systems or business mergers

<mark>INT, S/E When organizations interact, particularly on an international basis, there may be issues of software compatibility and language differences</mark>

"Here's your problem. The [illegible] manufactured in November and your computer was manufactured in February. Sagittarius is incompatible with Aquarius."

www.cartoonstock.com

- Both types involve compatibility issues since data from one system needs to be migrated to another usually old → new

- To preserve data integrity (no repetition or redundancy, no gaps, no corruption), the migration of data needs to ensure that data is not lost in the transfer/migration process

- This is another topic in which you can relate Opt A Databases to the current question

- Compatibility issues always arise when various databases (old & new, new & different) try to communicate with each other

- Loss of data because of brittle borders between legacy and new or between different systems is a serious area of concern

- Systems which are trying to communicate across language barriers have the added disadvantage of loss of characters in the transfer which sometimes may render data meaningless at the other end

1.1.4 Compare implementation of systems using client's hardware with hosting systems remotely

- (-) Client's hardware may need significant updating/renewal in order to cope with demands of new system
- (+) client's hardware is directly accessible on location and not remote therefore any services carried out can be done very quickly
- Hosting remotely ie SaaS (+) no license fees/ no responsibility for regular updates since all taken care of remotely
- (-) Severe reduction in security of data
- (-) Hosting system may be in different time zone → impacts running of system since systems are usually taken offline and 'serviced' during the small hours of the morning which may be peak business hours in another time zone
- Cloud computing and SaaS need to be very carefully considered by the management before any decisions are made to keep an organisation's data in a remote location

1.1.5 Evaluate alternative installation processes.

Students should be aware of the methods of implementation/ conversion. Parallel running, pilot running, direct changeover and phased conversion. S/E Training issues may require organizations to restructure their workforce

This is an evaluate topic so you need to be able to make valid points about each installation method. The context of the question is extremely important here. **Read it carefully before attempting to answer** since the method of installation which is suitable for one context may be completely wrong for another. Here are some very general guidelines (see exam questions practice for more specific scenarios):

1. **Parallel** running: **safe** since there is always a copy of processed data in old system in case new should fail. **Costly** since needs double manpower and man hours

2. **Pilot**: **relatively safe** since only one branch/department (contain the damage) usually smallest takes on the new system – if it fails other branches are not impacted. **Time** taken is longer since waiting for one branch to be declared successful before propagating to other branches.

3. **Direct** changeover: **relatively risky,** must have been tested very thoroughly to have gained nearly full confidence of users. **Relatively cheaper** since its put in place directly and **faster** – there is no waiting.

4. **Phased** conversion: **Each phase** of new system is put in place in a staggered manner to ensure it works successfully before implementing the next. **Safe but very cumbersome**. Likely to produce severe data bottlenecks and migration issues.

1.1.6 Discuss problems that may arise as part of data migration (moving data from system A to system B)

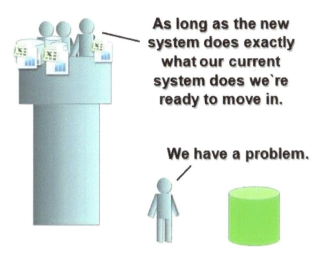

As long as the new system does exactly what our current system does we`re ready to move in.

We have a problem.

http://www.datamartist.com/data-migration-part-5-breaking-down-the-information-silos

Tips: This is a **discuss** topic so you must be making valid points for & against the question raised. You must also have a **valid conclusion** which is completely based on **your points discussed before!**

For this topic make sure you make reference to

You need to address various points on this including:

Inputting Data:

- Data formats
- Data structures
- Validation rules
- Incomplete data transfer
- International conventions on dates (dd/mm/yyyy vs mm/dd/yyyy)
- Currencies
- Character sets (Language eg. English → eg German and vice versa)

All of the above impact the migration of data in a negative way.

Processing Data:

- Will the migrated data be in a format ready to be processed
- How much pre-processing is required to get it into the correct format
- How much code needs to be modified, written anew for complete and correct processing of migrated data

Outputting: Will the data be 'at home' in the new environment and able to produce the required outputs eg sophisticated reports and calculations without too much extra processing.

==A very good topic to link to ETL in Opt A Databases!==

1.1.7 Suggest various types of testing

The crucial importance of testing at all stages of implementation should be emphasized, with the stages clearly defined.

Types of testing can include: user acceptance testing, debugging, beta testing.

Students should be aware that there are programs that can test other programs, thereby automating parts of the testing process and reducing costs.

S/E Inadequate testing can reduce employee productivity and lead to end-user dissatisfaction.

Again make reference to the magic Input → Processing → Output diagram!! This is at the heart of all you are learning in this science and must be referred to at every opportunity.

Read the question carefully – again the context is very important in the type of testing chosen.

Here are some basic guidelines (see Exam Questions for more contextual answers):

http://www.softwaretestingclass.com/what-is-manual-testing/

- All stages of implementation **must** involve testing – in most cases it is very useful to create a prototype with some basic input, processing and output functionality
- This prototype is then presented to the client for initial testing and feedback which is then used to modify and refine the various input, processing and output procedures

- The design phase of the system **must include a Testing Strategy** which shows that the engineers of the new system have seriously thought about all avenues of testing

- Input of data must cover validation testing: **typical**, **erroneous and boundary** data (not just a sample of each but **all foreseeable ranges**)

    E.g. DoB, suppose this is validated to accept values from of 01/01/1980 until 31/12/2010, then 15/07/2000 is **typical data**.

    The system should also accept the two boundary values 01/01/1980 and 31/12/2010. However, the system should reject 01/02/1962 with a valid and helpful error message that allows the user to make the correct choices

- Beta testing: depends very much on the type of system and some organisations may not wish to do this

- Acceptance testing (Testing system against user requirements, ie the requirement spec, and accepting point by point) – this is one of the most crucial types of testing when introducing a new system into an environment. The users are by far the most knowledgeable persons for feedback and their feedback must form the backbone of any further refinements of the system. It is after all their system and they must be able to trust it in order to work with it efficiently.

- Debugging (Fixing the code) – much of this can be avoided if in the design phase complete algorithms, pseudo-code , data flow diagrams and flow charts have been created. Algorithms and pseudocode, if traced correctly will save considerable time and effort later in debugging.

- When procedures and algorithms call other processes and algorithms in the code these should be tested in a hierarchical manner

- Insufficient testing: this can have disastrous results both for the employer and employees. In the first place if the employees are unable to trust the system due to insufficient testing they will not be able to work efficiently. Data may be lost, corrupted or misprocessed as a result. This corrupt data will then affect the customers which in turn will impact very negatively on the employer. Therefore there should be no cutting of costs or taking short cuts where testing is concerned.

- A range of users (beginner to advanced) must test the public 'face' of the system.

https://www.pinterest.com/pin/251146116690311774/

USER FOCUS

1.1.8 Describe the importance of user documentation

S/E The quality of user documentation can affect the rate of implementation of the new system.

This is a very controversial topic. Many users dislike reading user documentation! At the same time most users will probably need to refer to *some kind* of user documentation during the time they use a particular software system. But the title of this section, User Focus, implies that all should be 'seen' from the eyes of the User. More often than not, users do not possess sophisticated technical knowledge of the 'back-end' of the software system(s) they are using.

So the developers need to strike the right balance: creating easy to read but at the same time technical enough documentation which is easier said than done!

So why is user documentation important? Because:

- End users (or stake holders) need complete, easy-to-follow training manuals, tutorials and reference guides.
- We all need to undo mistakes sometimes
- If we need to alter the computer system some time down the line we need to be able to refer to the original documentation

In summary user documentation needs to be precise, up-to-date, easy to understand and in a format which is accessible to every type of user. The various formats will be discussed in the next section.

... taking great care "NOT" to press
the button labelled "Thermo-Nuclear War".

https://www.cartoonstock.com/directory/u/user_manual.asp

1.1.9 Evaluate different methods of providing user documentation

Examples should include methods such as: help files, online support and printed manuals.

S/E The quality of user documentation can affect the rate of implementation of the new system.

Historically user documentation took one form only: printed manuals! With the availability of online systems, it is now possible to have user documentation in a variety of formats:

- Brochures and flyers
- Newsletters
- Handouts and training aids
- User guides and manuals
- Online help systems
- E-mail and chat message:
- Web pages
- Proposals, letters, and memos
- Procedural and operational documentation
- Troubleshooting guides

Out of all the options above, web pages are probably the easiest and best for accessibility (24/7). They allow the user to go at their own pace and are usually supplemented with helpful hyperlinks and online 'chat' help.

Try to find some online user documentation by Microsoft and comment on its usefulness.

1.1.10 Evaluate different methods of delivering user training

Examples should include self-instruction, formal classes, remote/ online training.

S/E The quality of the delivery of user training can affect the rate of implementation of the new system

http://ethology.eu/can-two-training-methods-be-equally-good/

A summary of this excellent and in depth discussion of many different types of delivery is given below:

http://www.referenceforbusiness.com/management/Tr-Z/Training-Delivery-Methods.html

Formal classes – lecture method

The lecture is can be used to create a general understanding of a topic. During the pure lecture trainees listen, observe, and perhaps take notes.

Advantages	Disadvantages
• It can be useful in situations in which a large number of people must be given a limited amount of information in a relatively short period; • emphasis provided by trainer presentation skills to drive home important points • it is interactive, and that trainees can ask questions or have the presenter change the pace of the lecture if necessary	• it is not effective for learning large amounts of material in a short time period. • Trainees will forget information in direct proportion to the amount of information provided. • All trainees need to move at the pace of the presenter – some may find it difficult to keep up, others may be bored

Remote/online/eLearning

Many companies have implemented e-learning, which encompasses several different types of technology assisted training, such as distance learning, computer-based training (CBT), or web-based training (WBT).

Remote learning means trainers and trainees are in remote locations and use technology such as Skype or online live videos to broadcast a trainer's lecture to many trainees in many separate locations.

Main methods: content is delivered through the computer, using any combination of text, video, audio, chat rooms, or interactive assessment.

Distance learning provides many of the same advantages and disadvantages as the lecture method.

Advantages	Disadvantages
<ul><li>**reduce trainee learning time, by allowing trainees to progress at their own pace**</li><li>**reduce the cost of training, particularly by reducing costs associated with travel to a training location**</li><li>**provide instructional consistency, by offering the same training content to employees worldwide**</li><li>**allow trainees to learn at their own pace thereby reducing any boredom or anxiety that may occur**</li><li>**provide a safe method for learning hazardous tasks with computer simulations**</li><li>**increase access to training to learners in locations around the world**</li></ul>	<ul><li>Reduced motivation to learn due to physical absence of trainer</li><li>no opportunity during e-learning to discuss attitudes with others in a setting where a trainer can monitor, direct, and reinforce the discussion to support the desired attitude(s).</li></ul>

In many cases adult learners indicate a preference for e-learning to be combined with some form of instructor-based training – this is called 'blended training', which is when both computer and face-to-face training are combined, and it is used by many organizations.

Self instruction

In many cases, stake holders may decide that they wish to go through the training process on their own. This is usually stake holders who are more comfortable with learning at their own pace rather than following a group's learning routine. The individual can then complete the training in their own time, however, the main drawback in this case is the application of self-discipline. Unless the stake holder is very good with managing their time and schedule, often the training gets pushed back and is never completed.

SYSTEM BACKUP

1.1.11 Identify a range of causes of data loss.

Causes include malicious activities and natural disasters.

S/E Malicious activity may be a result of activities by employees within the organization or intruders.

Loss of data, particularly of *master files* can have serious effects on an organisation

Obviously the larger the organisation and the more sensitive the nature of the files lost, the more serious the effects

The main causes of data loss are categorised as follows:

- Environmental hazards such as fire, flood, and other natural accidents
- Mechanical problems such as the danger of the back up disk or tape being damaged by a drive malfunction
- Software problems caused by programming error
- Human error – loading the wrong file, using the wrong version of a program, mislaid hardware used for backup, physical damage

- Malicious damage – staff intentionally damaging storage media or misusing programs at their terminals

1.1.12 Outline the consequences of data loss in a specified situation

S/E Loss of medical records, cancellation of a hotel reservation without the knowledge of the traveller.

The results of data loss can be catastrophic, and an industry study carried out by the Diffusion Group finds that 72 per cent of businesses that suffer a significant loss of data close their doors within two years.

The financial effects of data loss can be hard to recover from, with costs incurred coming from fines for improper management of customer information, the costs of repairing the breach, and potential compensation payouts to customers.

The cost to a business' reputation can be greater still, and even harder to recover from. Whether consumers or business clients, customers put trust in a company to keep their information safe, and if that trust is broken, their belief and trust in the company can quickly evaporate.

In situations where confidential company data is lost or stolen, it can severely harm the competitiveness and credibility of the business, and the belief of any business partners.

1.1.13 Describe a range of methods that can be used to prevent data loss.

These should include failover systems, redundancy, removable media, offsite/online storage.

Unfortunately, data breaches are far from a rare occurrence. A blog on the Guardian Newspaper Media Network reveals that 78 per cent of organisations have experienced at least one data breach in the past two years, while 60 per cent of small and medium-sized enterprises admit to not routinely backing up data.

Malware, email attacks and phishing scams are identified as the most common causes of external data loss, and 36 per cent of the lost data was either customer information or financial data.

To help ensure a business does not become a part of these statistics, companies and organisations need to take steps to proactively prevent data breaches and data loss.

So, what needs to be done?

1. Install effective virus/malware protection and firewalls

This is the most basic level of defence that all organisations, whether large or small, should vigorously put in place.

Having a virus/malware protection solution that is robust and up to date is absolutely imperative and will do a significant amount to prevent unauthorised access to your data or its destruction by malevolent software.

All devices should have the same level of security, whether desktop PCs, laptops, tablets or smartphones.

2. Change passwords often

Passwords become less effective at securing systems and data the longer they remain unchanged; they can be shared or exposed through sheer negligence, or stolen via technological methods such as hacking or through social manipulation.

By changing all passwords across the organisation frequently, the company is effectively reducing the risks of unauthorised access. Best practice is to change passwords every 2-3 months, and those passwords which provide access to more sensitive data should be changed most frequently.

3. Create specific and tailored data protection policies

Though the technological efforts of cyber intruders present a considerable risk, the actions (and inaction) of employees should not be overlooked when considering how data might be lost or stolen.

By creating formal policy documents for protecting data and ensuring that all stake holders are aware and have signed these policies upon joining the organisation, the risks can be significantly reduced since stake holders are made aware of the legal and criminal consequences of maliciously tampering with data held by the organisation.

4. Secure document formats

Data is only ever as secure as the documents it's contained within, whether it's text or numerical data. PDF files can be a particularly secure way of storing and sharing documents, as they can be encrypted and password-protected to prevent unauthorised access, copying and printing.

By using professional PDF software, such as Power PDF, solutions you can integrate these capabilities into your existing document management system, as well as enabling the digital signatures and redacting confidential information for additional security.

5. Securing the print network and practices

It's not just information stored digitally which can be compromised. Once data is printed out what happens to it? There are several possible data loss risks associated with printing, namely

- Sensitive printouts being forgotten about and left at the printer
- Printouts being lost or misplaced within the office or outside of it
- Unauthorised printing of confidential information

To protect against these risks the organisation should consider utilising software-based print management solutions which make it possible to control who is printing, require that they be at the printer itself to release the print job, and keep track of who is printing what.

Finally, in a world where employees are increasingly working from home or another external location, be sure to take steps to ensure that all of the devices that they use are as secure as in the office itself.

6. Cloud computing & Data Management

With the advent of cloud computing some years ago stake holders found it more 'fashionable' to store their data on a remote server. The top risks have been identified by one security company as follows:

http://www.calyptix.com/research-2/top-5-risks-of-cloud-computing/

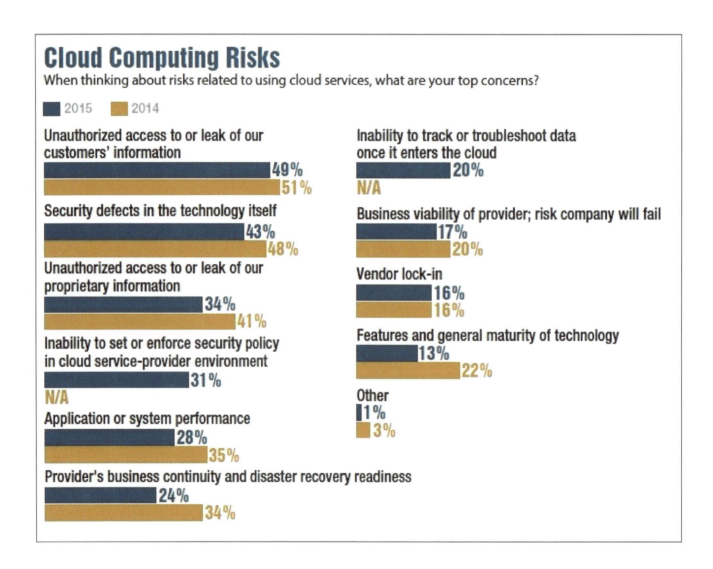

SOFTWARE DEPLOYMENT

1.1.14 Describe strategies for managing releases and updates

Once upon a time a major telecommunications provider had a problem. It needed to implement a business critical supplier switch, which required it to reengineer its billing and account management systems. These systems had to be in place within three months, otherwise the organization risked losing hundreds of millions of pounds and a decline in their stock value. But the telecom's development processes were poor, and its release management was extremely problematic and inconsistent.

In a very engaging story written by By Mike Sutton and Tym Moore (http://www.cio.com/article/2434640/developer/7-ways-to-improve-your-software-release-management.html?page=2) they discuss how these problems were overcome. The summary is below:

1. Understand the current state of release management.

Establish a detailed picture of the current release process using fact-finding methods and interview techniques with key individuals – this is a link to what you learnt in a previous topic.

Discover the state of the Test environments - if they are limited and not managed, then they will be out of date and not usable.

2. Establish a regular release cycle.

"If the engineering team is the heart of the project, the release cycle is its heartbeat".

Establishing a release cycle is vital because:

1. It creates an opportunity to meaningfully discuss nonfunctional testing that the software may need.

2. It announces a timetable for when stakeholders can expect to get some functionality. If they know that functionality will be regularly released, they can get on with agreeing what that functionality will be.

3. It creates a routine with which all teams can align (including marketing and engineering).

4. It gives customers confidence that they can order something and it will be delivered.

Before announcing the release cycle it must be tested out. There is nothing worse for a failing release process than more unrealistic dates!

The most important point is that the company should be able to deliver the desired level of quality – the customers are happy to wait for this.

3. Review the documentation regularly!

Here is a summary of how professionals carry out the process:

> ➢ Assign a sequence of tasks to release the software from the engineering teams.

- Do a dry run, using dummy code for each element.
- Test the sequence, documenting what was done
- This formed the basis of the installation instructions.
- Now the deployment team (see Software Deployment section) perform another dry run, using *this new* documentation. They extend, amend and improved the current documentation.
- Review the process after each release.
- Examine the documentation, identify changes made during the release.
- Update the documentation!

4. Establish a release infrastructure early.

Release infrastructure means anything that needs to be in place to deploy the software and to enable users to use it. The obligation to the customer is not just that you build great software; it is that it's available for them to access and use.

Crucial to getting a good release process is figuring out what you need to have in place to make it available to the customer—*before* the engineering team is done building the software.

The release infrastructure covers the hardware, storage, network connections, bandwidth, software licenses, user profiles and access permissions.

Human services and skills are part of the release infrastructure, too. For example, if you require specialist software installed and configured, it's not smart to exclude the availability or cost of getting such skills into your infrastructure plan.

It is critical to discover, as early as possible, hidden bottlenecks in obtaining the required hardware or the missing skills (say, to configure secure networks so that delivery is not delayed.

This isn't trivial and in the real world it is often the cause of serious delays.

5. Automate and standardize as much as possible

Automation (one of the two pillars of Computing) enables us to have machines carry repetitive tasks without tying up valuable human resources. Standardizing ensures that automation's inputs and outputs are consistent every time.

http://www.slideshare.net/fovak/funny-cartoons-1084389

1.2 System design basics

1.2.1 Define the terms: hardware, software, peripheral, network, human resources.

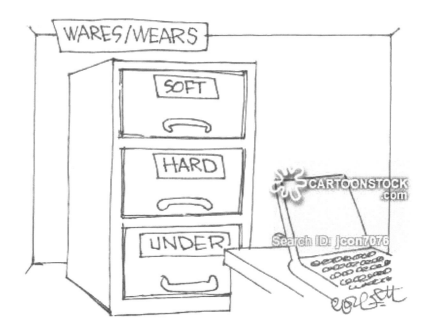

Hardware: Any physical component of a computer system which can be touched eg mouse, printer, monitor, hard drive.

Software: Any single or collection of computer programs (code) which are used in applications or Operating Systems eg Word processing, Spreadsheet software, Windows OS

Peripheral: Any devices which are in the 'periphery' or 'vicinity' of a computer or computer system eg printers, scanners, cameras

Network: A collection of two or more computers which are connected either by physical cables or by a wireless connection

1.2.2 Describe the roles that a computer can take in a networked world.

Roles include client, server, email server, DNS server, router and firewall.

A physical computer serves one or more people, either at home, or in an organisation or company. If this computer is being used by a 'User' of the system in a network then it is referred to as a 'client' computer.

If the computer is very powerful and with a large amount of storage space and it is used in a network for example to serve the users with all their files then it is termed a 'File Server'. Server computers have many different roles eg mail server, print server

A DNS or Domain Network Server:

A **DNS server** is any computer registered to join the Domain Name System. A **DNS server** runs special-purpose networking software, features a public IP address, and contains a database of network names and addresses for other Internet hosts

The purpose of a **router** is to connect a computer to the world wide web. If the computer is in a network then there is also need for gateways as well as routers in order to 'translate' the protocol of the local network into Internet Protocol (IP).

A **firewall** can be hardware, software or both and consists of filters and physical components which are designed to prevent unauthorized **access** to or from a private PC or network.

Hardware and Software Firewalls

Firewalls can be either hardware or software but the ideal will consist of both. In addition to limiting access to your computer and network, a firewall is also useful for allowing remote access to a private network through secure authentication certificates and logins.

Hardware firewalls can be purchased as a stand-alone product but are also typically found in broadband routers, and should be considered an important part of your system and network set-up. Software firewalls are installed on your computer (like any software) and are customisable, allowing you some control over its function and protection features. A software firewall will protect your computer from outside attempts to control or gain access your computer.

"And just why would you need a firewall?"

1.2.3 Discuss the social and ethical issues associated with a networked world.

AIM 8, AIM 9 Develop an appreciation of the social and ethical issues associated with continued developments in computer systems.

Computer ethics are a set of principles which try to regulate the use of computers. There are 3 major factors to be considered:

1. **Intellectual Property Rights** – this covers the copying of software without the permission of the owner

2. **Privacy Issues** – this includes hacking or any illegal access to another person's personal data

3. **Effect of computers on society** – this considers factors such as job losses and social impacts on people and their methods of interaction.

Systems Analysis & Design

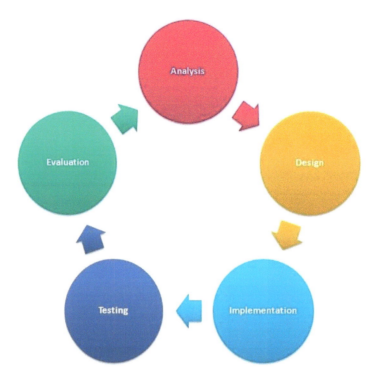

http://nathanlunn.com/wp-content/uploads/2013/08/SDLC.jpg

1.2.3 Identify the relevant stakeholders when planning a new system.

S/E The role of the end-user must   be considered when planning a new system.

Who is a relevant stakeholder?

TOK Utilitarianism, the greatest good for the greatest number. The means justify the ends.

The relevant stakeholders are the persons who use a computer system and its component applications in a school, business or other organisation.

When a team of System Analysts visit such a business or organisation with a view to implementing a new system they need to carry out a thorough analysis of the user needs.

Four methods of analysis are used: Interview, Observation, Questionnaire and study of relevant documentation.

It is only through a combination of one or more of these techniques that that the role of the **relevant stakeholders** or users of the system/s becomes more clear and as a result the

Analysts are better able to instruct the team of designers on what they need to be designing to meet the needs of the stake holders.

Who is a relevant stakeholder? A person/team of persons whose job has a specific set of functionalities using computer software. For example an accountant in a school, a registrar in an office, a student, a Principal, a company CEO. Each of these has vastly different requirements and is considered a relevant stakeholder of their organisation or company.

1.2.5 Describe methods of obtaining requirements from stakeholders.

Including surveys, interviews, direct observations.

AIM 5 The need for effective collaboration to obtain appropriate information from stakeholders.

S/E The question of privacy for stakeholders.

"Taking his job as Systems Analyst a bit literally, isn't he?"

http://www.modernanalyst.com/Portals/0/Public%20Uploads/Fin414-Systems-Analyst.jpg

As mentioned in the previous section there are four methods at the disposal of system analysts in order to collect enough information to produce a design for a new computer system.

The main objective here is to find out from the **outside in** how a given computer system is working. So the obvious answer would be to try and use all four methods.

Method	Advantages	Disadvantages
Survey/Questionnaire	o **Fast to produce** o **Fast to collate results** o **Short questions/multiple choice answers**	o **Quite shallow in what it reveals** o **Answers may not be adequate to form a good picture of the system**
Interview	▪ **Direct and 1-2-1 with stakeholders** ▪ **Can be quite revealing and helpful depending on the stakeholder and their role**	▪ **Some stakeholders react quite negatively to interviews and 'clam up' in case their job might be in jeopardy** ▪ **They may reveal insufficient information**
Observation	❖ **The most reliable method of finding out exactly what each stakeholder uses the system for** ❖ **Gives a good idea of the range of uses of the system**	❖ **Can be quite time consuming** ❖ **Analyst may not be able to cover a wide enough range of stakeholders in their given time constraints**
Documentation	➢ **A reliable method of collecting information** ➢ **Shows depth/detail of the system providing the documentation is complete**	➢ **It very much depends on whether there is *any* documentation to speak of or not** ➢ **Any updates to the system if not documented will produce an incomplete 'view' of the system**

1.2.6 Describe appropriate techniques for gathering the information needed to arrive at a workable solution.

Examining current systems, competing products, organizational capabilities, literature searches.

S/E Intellectual property.

This specification point is exactly the same as the previous one so see above!

1.2.7 Construct suitable representations to illustrate system requirements.

Examples include: system flow charts, data flow diagrams, structure chart.

UML is not required.

LINK Flow chart symbols, flow charts and pseudocode.

Once the systems analysts have collected enough information on the roles & requirements of the stake holders they will produce a document known as the **Requirements Specification** which sets out in detail what is required in order to make the new system.

"Based on our tests, the business stakeholders fall asleep around page 37 of the Functional Requirements Specification. Put the Issues Section on page 40."

https://s-media-cache-ak0.pinimg.com/originals/cb/ff/e8/cbffe82f4ec4de731994accee8a86fed.jpg

This requirement specification is then handed to the **Design Team** who will produce the design of the new system based on the following:

Abstraction:

Abstraction is the process of removing unnecessary detail in order to find out exactly what problem needs to be solved.

Algorithm:

Once it is clear what the problem is to be solved, an **algorithm** or step by step set of instructions needs to be produced on how to solve the set of tasks involved.

There are two methods for producing algorithms: **flow charts or pseudocode**

Each method has its advantages and at the end of the design process it should be able to use *either* in order to **automate** the solution.

Automation:

This is the process of turning the flowchart or pseudocode for each module of the new system into code (any programming language of choice by the Implementation Team).

The implementation team will now code the solution – at times there may be large numbers of teams working on various modules of the system. These are then put together in order to produce a **prototype**. The purpose of the prototype is to find out how much of the stakeholders requirements have actually been implemented correctly. This is discussed in the next section.

1.2.8 Describe the purpose of prototypes to demonstrate the proposed system to the client.

AIM 5 The need to effectively collaborate to gather appropriate information to resolve complex problems.

AIM 6 To develop logical and critical thinking to develop proposed systems.

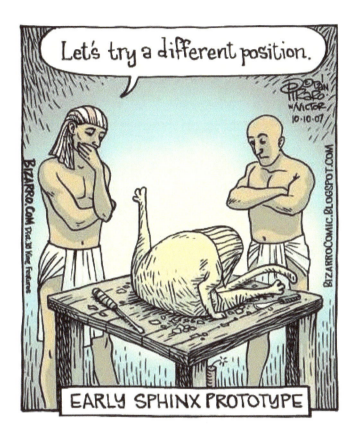

https://s-media-cache-ak0.pinimg.com/736x/4b/38/04/4b38048dbf098bbf20f0499bf69d505e.jpg

The most important purpose served by prototypes is to find out whether it is what the stakeholders wanted or not! This model will then be tweaked (see iteration below) in order to fine tune the solution.

There may be more than one prototype involved in a new system – one per module depending on the various requirements of each module. These prototypes are put into use by the stakeholders in order to verify their functionality. The advantages and disadvantages of the prototypes need to be carefully documented and this will in turn go back to the design team who will tweak the concepts in order to better serve the stakeholders requirements. See iteration below.

1.2.9 Discuss the importance of iteration during the design process.

Iterative design is a **design** methodology based on a cyclic process of prototyping, testing, analyzing, and refining a product or process.

Based on the results of testing the most recent **iteration** of a **design**, changes and refinements are made.

At each testing phase of the prototype new suggestions by users are taken on board and incorporated into refining the prototype's design. These refinements are then incorporated into a later version of the prototype and testing and further refinements follow.

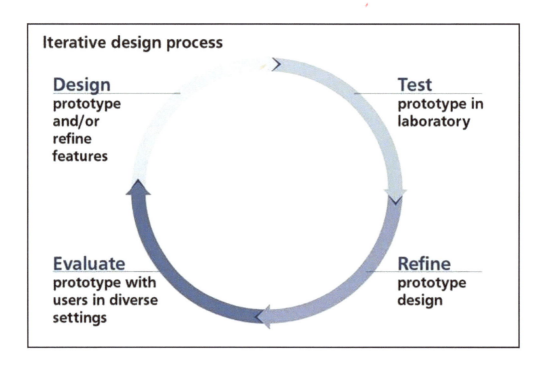

1.2.10 Explain the possible consequences of failing to involve the end-user in the design process.

S/E The failure to involve the end-user may lead to software that is not suitable for its intended use, which may have adverse effects on user productivity.

AIM 5 The need for effective collaboration and communication between the client, developer and end-user.

It is a very well-known reality that the whole process of the Systems Life Cycle from pre-Analysis up to Testing & Evaluation is hardly ever a fail-proof procedure. Many teams are involved in the creation of the new system from inception to completion. Lack of sufficient communication between teams, lack of enough detail in the Analysis phase, lack of sufficient documentation and many other factors contribute to a solution in many cases, which is hardly what the stakeholder required at all! It is therefore absolutely crucial to have as many of the end-users or stakeholders involved in the process of analysis and design as possible in order to produce a Requirement Specification which matches very closely what they all require. **Of course it is not always possible to give every end-user exactly what they wish!** Compromises must be made and these are very much as a result of time or budget constraints. But failing to include the end-users at all would be a disastrous course to follow since the team carrying out the analysis phase are absolutely dependent on their input (no pun intended!)

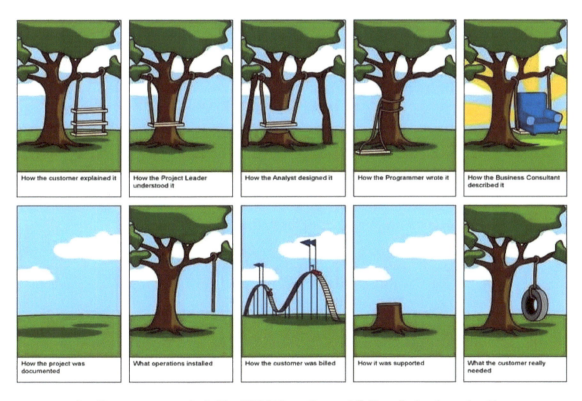

http://www.uxmatters.com/mt/archives/2011/04/images/ia-summit/fig23_quality-iterations_reduced.jpg

1.2.11 Discuss the social and ethical issues associated with the introduction of new IT systems.

AIM 8, **AIM 9** Develop an appreciation of the social and ethical issues associated with continued developments in specified computer systems

Human interaction with the system

Also known ask Human Computer Interface (HCI)

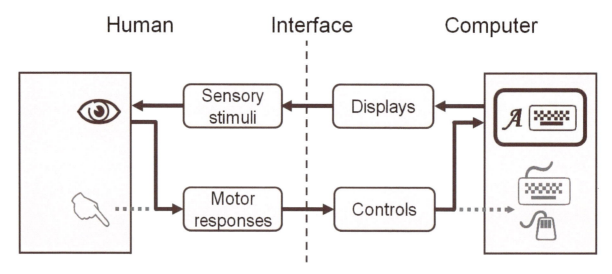

http://www.yorku.ca/mack/cogain-f2.jpg

1.2.12 Define the term usability.

S/E This includes ergonomics and accessibility.

Usability describes the extent to which a device is **usable** by a designated set of users. These users may have very specific requirements such as those who need specific input/output devices in order to overcome various types of disabilities.

1.2.13 Identify a range of usability problems with commonly used digital devices.

S/E Students should be aware of usability issues in a range of devices including PCs, digital cameras, cell phones, games consoles, MP3 players and other commonly used digital devices.

A very general specification point covering a huge range but only requiring you to identify the problems. A good exercise is to complete the following table with everyone in your class contributing to at least one of the devices. These problems are very user specific and the completion of this table will give you a better picture of the recurring problems across the various devices:

Device	Usability problems
PC	Input: Keyboard, mouse Output: on screen, on paper Problems:
Digital Camera	
Cell phone	
Game consoles	
MP3 players	
Other devices	

Use the following diagram to help you fill the table above.

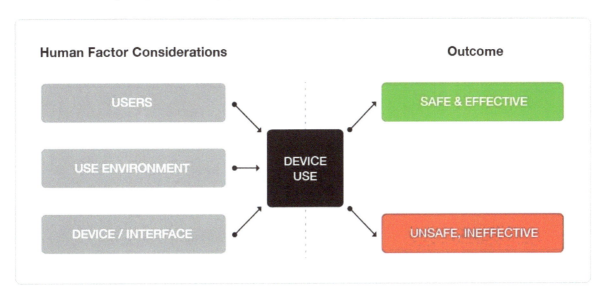

http://medical-device-usability.com/wp-content/uploads/2015/04/device-use.jpg

1.2.14 Identify methods that can be used to improve the accessibility of systems.

S/E Examples include touch screen, voice recognition, text-to-speech, Braille keyboard.

This is very much an I.T specification point as opposed to a Computer Science specification point. It is asking you to identify the ways in which the *'standard'* input-output devices can be improved in order to help those with specific disabilities. Again, it is a good class exercise and you can find a very good place to learn here:

http://www.teachict.com/gcse_computing/ocr/212_computing_hardware/disabled_ipop/miniweb/index.php

1.2.15 Identify a range of usability problems that can occur in a system.

S/E These should be related to the systems.

Systems include ticketing, online payroll, scheduling, voice recognition, systems that provide feedback.

Every one of the systems included in this specification point ie ticketing, online payroll, scheduling, voice recognition etc use a database or information management system at the back-end in order to perform various tasks. Each type of system has its own specific type of usability problems but in essence these are all about the insertion, deletion, update of date into a database as well as querying the database for various reporting purposes. This specification point does not require you to discuss any of these problems but simply to identify a range of them.

This is very much an investigative point – try to create a 'flipped' lesson around this specification point. You can interview students & staff in your school for these problems by creating a simple questionnaire on https://www.surveymonkey.co.uk/

Next collate the results and insert into a table similar to the one in Section 1.2.13. In this way you will have a number of examples at your fingertips straight from stakeholders!

1.2.16 Discuss the moral, ethical, social, economic and environmental implications of the interaction between humans and machines.

AIM 8 Raise awareness of the moral, ethical, social, economic and environmental implications of using science and technology.

As a **Discuss** point this topic carries much weight and you can be sure that there will be an examination question on this topic, which will be 'wrapped' in the context of a business or organisation of some kind. As a discuss topic, this one is NOT for private study! Attempt each of the categories below in your class with your classmates. Create mind maps, presentations, flow charts and even movie clips to get your points across.

Issue	What it means	Description
Moral	Factors that define how an individual acts and behaves	Moral issues concern our individual behaviour and personal concept of right & wrong We learn moral values from parents, teachers and peers. Later on in life, we learn them for ourselves from experience and study. Some argue that there is no right or wrong with moral issues – that it is all a matter of personal preference. **Discuss in class – create a mind map or presentation showing various sides of this argument.**
Ethical	Factors that define the set of moral values by which society functions	Some people argue that even actions that are illegal might still be ethical. One of the main issues is the widespread collection and use or misuse of personal data by 3rd parties. **Discuss using Personal privacy, Data security, misuse of data, Big Brother, Online profiling**
Social	Factors which affect us as members of a society	Unauthorised access by hackers Unauthorised use of software Inappropriate behaviour Inappropriate content Freedom of speech Unemployment Access to the Internet across the globe – the digital divide **Discuss in groups using examples from 1st world vs 3rd world countries.**
Economic	Factors that affect the economic status of the society we live in	**Discuss:** Unemployment caused by automation vs the creation of new jobs which did not exist before the Information Age eg Web Designers, Big Data Analysts
Environmental	Factors that affect the environment in which we live	**Are there any environmental benefits to a digital life?** For example, online shopping, working remotely from home, teleconferencing are all factors which can be seen as having a **positive** environmental effect since they reduce the need for travel, use of fuel and pollution. The down side of this argument could be the new 'mountain' of digital waste which our generation is leaving behind. Admittedly some of this digital waste is being recycled and used in 3rd world countries but these countries are very quickly catching up and soon will be creating their own digital waste to match ours! **Discuss.**

www.ingramcontent.com/pod-product-compliance
Lightning Source LLC
Chambersburg PA
CBHW041432050326
40690CB00002B/516